How to Respond to . . . THE CULTS

Hubert F. Beck

Publishing House
St. Louis

THE RESPONSE SERIES

How to Respond to the Cults
How to Respond to Transcendental Meditation
How to Respond to the Lodge
How to Respond to the Latter Day Saints
How to Respond to the Occult
How to Respond to Jehovah's Witnesses

Concordia Publishing House, St. Louis, Missouri
Copyright © 1977 Concordia Publishing House
Manufactured in the United States of America

Library of Congress Cataloging in Publication Data

Beck, Herbert F
    How to respond to . . . the cults.

    (Response series)
    Bibliography: p.
    1. Cults—United States. I. Title.
BL2530.U6B4   200'.973   77-23815
ISBN 0-570-07682-X

6 7 8 9 10 11 12 13 14 15 SB 89 88 87 86 85 84 83 82 81 80

Foreword to the Response Series

This series of booklets serves as a response to the need expressed by the members of The Lutheran Church—Missouri Synod assembled in national convention at Anaheim, Calif., July 1975, for specialized literature to assist in the "evangelization of persons who belong to anti-Christian sects and cults."

Those who were responsible for responding to that need, which the convention put into a formal resolution, called on others to explore the need further. The result was the development of this series of booklets. It was felt that the need was best summed up by St. Peter when he advised Christians "always be ready to answer anyone who asks you to explain the hope you have, but be gentle and respectful" (1 Peter 3:15 Beck).

In today's society, where cults, sects, and movements have multiplied, it is often difficult for the Christian to feel confident that he is "ready to answer." This series is planned to help the Christian in that dilemma by providing him information about cults by comparing the teachings of cults with the Christian faith.

Some of the cults are very evangelistic, seeking to make converts of everyone who will listen. This series also seeks to help the Christian share his faith with those who seek to evangelize him, and to do so in a "gentle and respectful" way, as Peter suggests. For that reason each of the books not only seeks to compare the basic teachings of the cult with Christianity but suggests how to witness to its members.

The booklets are intended to be used in two ways. They can be read and studied by an individual who is confronted with a specific need to know about one cult, or they can be studied in a series by a Bible study group. The series is introduced by the "foundation" book, which provides an overview of "cult mentality" and the more general problems posed by cults in our culture. The series continues with selecting some of the larger or more influential groups for coverage in a specific booklet.

The series begins with the foundation booklet and five specific ones. It is hoped that, after the successful acceptance of this first issue by the church, other specific booklets can be added, dealing with those cults that are for the moment of most concern to Christian people.

Erwin J. Kolb, *Executive Secretary*
The Board for Evangelism
The Lutheran Church—Missouri Synod

Editor's Preface

The Rev. Hubert F. Beck serves as campus pastor to Lutheran students at Texas A & M University, College Station, Tex. In his campus ministry he encounters people who are not only involved in many Christian denominations, but also in cults, sects, and alternative life-styles of every description.

Pastor Beck sees the church as C. W. Brister defines it, "a community of Christians who care for one another and seek by varied means to extend that care to persons outside the church" (*People Who Care,* page 75). His concern is that people committed to Jesus Christ may communicate by their words and actions the Gospel of God's saving grace in His Son.

In the final section of this little volume, Pastor Beck impresses on his readers that they are always to be learners as well as teachers, and he points them to the source of all truth, the Holy Scriptures.

When used alone or together with other specific booklets in this series, Pastor Beck's "foundation" book addresses itself to that familiar feeling, "I wish I had said something . . ." after someone has knocked on our door and gone away.

May this little volume help us all to "always be ready to answer anyone who asks you to explain the hope you have, but be gentle and respectful."

Philip Lochhaas, *Executive Secretary*
The Commission on Organizations
The Lutheran Church—Missouri Synod

Contents

1

Characteristics of Cults

Introduction

"A cult is a religious perversion. It is a belief and practise in the world of religion which calls for devotion to a religious view or leader centered in false doctrine. It is an organized heresy."

With these words Dave Breese defines a cult in his book *Know the Marks of Cults.*

"By the term 'cult' I mean nothing derogatory to any group so classified. A cult, as I define it, is any religious group which differs significantly in some one or more respects as to belief or practise, from those religious groups which are regarded as the normative expressions of religion in our total culture."

This is the way Dr. Charles Braden defines a cult in *These Also Believe* as quoted by Walter Martin. Mr. Martin then adds these comments:

"I may add to this that a cult might also be defined as a group of people gathered about a specific person or person's interpretation of the Bible." This becomes the subject of considerable elaboration in Mr. Martin's book *The Kingdom of the Cults.*

This sampling of definitions will alert the reader to the fact that there are broad definitions of the word cult commonly accepted and at the same time there is some difficulty in pinning down specifically what the dividing line is between terms like cult and sect or even a denomination as compared to a cult or sect.

Our discussion in this booklet and those to follow will focus more specifically on cults as religious groups that have deviated so significantly from the religious thought and norms that gave them birth as to have become a *new* and *altered* stream of faith and life.

It should be noted that we have not specifically said they are deviations from *Christian* orthodoxy and norms, for many contemporary cults have been born of religious frames of reference other than Christian. Religious beliefs of the Baha'is, Black Muslims, and Anglo-Israelis are all altered forms of religious thought other than Christian, but would still be considered cults by the definition here in use.

A cult, then, cannot be considered merely a peripheral statement of an original faith pattern compared to a sect which at least marginally participates in the basic faith within which it has its roots. A cult takes its point of departure from the religious thought of a major religion, but twists and warps that pattern of faith until it has become something essentially new and different from what it was originally.

Cults—The Unpaid Bills of the Church

It has been said that "the cults are the unpaid bills of the church." (Dr. Van Baalen, quoted by Walter Martin in *The Kingdom of the Cults.*)

There is, indeed, much truth to this assertion. That is one reason they can confuse Christians so easily. Cult members speak against a broad and knowledgeable background, since they know very well what orthodox thought is. They use language that people rooted in major faith systems recognize and understand. It is difficult to sort out where the recognizable terminologies end and the heretical manipulations of thought begin. People hear familiar and strange things at the same time and don't know what to make of it.

In the worst sense of the term, then, the cults are schismatic and heretical, for they freely use terminology and phraseology that is typical of their parent background. Their words are, however, constantly filled with new and different understandings, quite far from the original meaning.

Examples of twisting words and phrases can be found among Jehovah's Witnesses, who speak of "everlasting death" as "annihilation" (denying the resurrection of all flesh), "hell" as "the common grave of mankind" (with subsequent denial of God's wrath), and "Jesus Christ" as "a created individual; a god" (but denying in the process His coequality with the Father and the Holy Spirit and His participation in the eternal Godhead). Such twisting of terms occurs over and over. It becomes so misleading and confusing that one almost despairs of seriously understanding what is happening in conversation.

The church has a serious responsibility toward the cults. In some way to church needs to engage in dialog with the cults to challenge them in their use of terms, to witness to the full force of those terms in their original and continuing usage in the church, and to once more call the adherents of the cults to a meaningful response to the message and mission of the church.

In many other ways to be suggested throughout this pamphlet the cults are "unpaid bills of the church." In this area of terminology alone, the church is challenged by the cults to clarify its own intention and message. This need dare not go unheeded.

The Mentality of the Cults

Quite obviously there is no one umbrella under which all cults may be placed. One must be careful not to overgeneralize. Yet there are some positions that are found commonly enough among the cults that we can speak of a "mentality of the cults."

The doctrine of the last days and the last things will often appear in their teachings. This is frequently attached to warnings that point to contemporary signs of the impending end of the world. An example of such a stress on eschatology (the formal word for the doctrine of the latter days of the world) can be found with the stress on the thousand years' reign of Jehovah as is found among Jehovah's Witnesses. This stress on latter days and signs of the end is a frequent overlap between teaching of the cults and some sectarian teachings of groups that remain marginal to the major faith systems. It is not exclusive to the cults themselves.

Prophecy and fulfillment is another point of overlap between sectarian concerns and the teachings of the cults. An extremity of this emphasis is found in Anglo-Israelism (known as British-Israelism in England). Pointing to selected prophecies and fulfillment occasionally exerts tremendous influence on people, since it has a familiar ring.

Priestly authority may be stressed a great deal in some cults, particularly if a system of secret rituals and symbols is involved. An example of this emphasis can be found in The Church of Jesus Christ of Latter-day Saints.

Among *occult* groups, forms of Gnosticism, a set of inner secrets leading to saving knowledge to be shared only with the initiated, may well appear. This may be coupled with the sort of priestly authority mentioned above and may give rise to castes and structures of authority to preserve the "mysteries" intact. Thus they can be passed from generation to generation.

Most cults are very dogmatic. Consequently they are highly intolerant of deviations from their teachings and life. There appear to be significant exceptions to this in bodies such as Baha'i which asserts a high tolerance for a variety of ideas and opinions in order to become a gathering place for all religions. Upon closer inspection, however, tolerance disappears very quickly as one moves to the heart of their beliefs.

Appearance of tolerance usually is found among cults with Eastern religions as their foundation, but in many instances it proves to be only on the surface. The exception may be in freethinking societies such as the Unitarian-Universalists, although there, too, one may be bewildered by a sudden appearance of rather dogmatic pronouncements and a refusal to tolerate divergent opinions.

In many instances the cults base their claims on the supernatural, with special revelations from God as their touchstone for authority. Special revelation is nearly always tied to a particular leader who received such revelations. This is part of what makes dialog with cults difficult, for if there is indeed a special revelation given to a particular leader, there is no argument that can be "reasonably" raised. "Reason" is not part of the total picture, and all discussion becomes authoritative.

In keeping with special "revelations" the cults are convinced that their "way" will be proved in the end. Exceptions to such an anticipation of "victory" are found in followers of Transcendental Meditation and similar groups, since they have no "end" or "proof" or "victory" in sight other than the satisfaction one derives from their meditative processes at the moment.

A sense of sin is frequently either minimized or totally absent in the cults. Resisting the cults or living outside their purview might be thought of as sin by them, but in the traditional sense sin does not appear as a deep concern.

The idea of salvation, then, takes on different meanings also. It is generally related to maintaining stability throughout one's lifetime or else is translated into an ephemeral other world at a future time. It does not necessarily tie itself to relationship to God as much as to membership and participation in the cult itself.

With this idea of salvation underlying their existence, it is not surprising to find the leaders or founders of such cults filling a sort of "messianic" or "saving" office for the cults. Salvation becomes tied to the founder or a subsequent leader of the cult, whether that claim was there originally or not.

There is a tendency in most cults to stress nonessentials and relatively minor matters so that these assume a central place. Jehovah's Witnesses, e.g., have some very strong central thrusts in their faith, but issues such as blood transfusions and the oath of allegiance to the flag become so tied to these thrusts that on occasion they take on more importance than they were intended to have. Christians sometimes mistake these relatively minor matters as the essential points of difference and do not understand what the primary concern is about. To argue the ethical rightness of blood transfusion with a Jehovah's Witness may be an interesting diversion, but it does not touch on the heart of the concerns of either a Christian or a Jehovah's Witness.

Rarely, if ever, would all of the above be found in one cult, but there are some distinguishing features common to all cults.

There is, e.g., an almost universal tendency among the cults to assign much authoritative power to a leader, a headquarters, a basic belief system that may not be challenged. They have a basic set of presuppositions underlying their position, and in almost every instance it is of vital importance to uncover that set of presuppositions before one can speak seriously with them. That is part of the task of this series of booklets—to help uncover the presuppositions within various cults.

A form of "double talk" runs through the entire thought systems of the cults. It is virtually universal that they have a special vocabulary, although the vocabulary itself will not be universal—even among the various cults as you go from one to the other! Each cult has its own unique vocabulary. One cannot assume knowledge of one cult by mastering the conceptual framework of another cult. That, too, is part of the task of this series of booklets—to help differentiate and particularize the vocabulary and phraseology of each cult. At the same time one must realize that what a word means to you is by no means what the same word may mean to a cult member. It is this difficulty of mastering what a cult means by its vocabulary that makes dialog so difficult.

Another universal mark to be noted is a complete lack of interest in logical consistency. Although all of us undoubtedly lack logical consistency in certain areas of our thinking, members of the cults are very adept at doing mental flip-flops that bewilder the average person. This further makes dialog with them difficult, for it is frequently at the most crucial junctures that they are guilty of the greatest *in*consistency. When this is drawn to their attention it only serves to convince them that the listener has "not seen the light" and is therefore still closed to the "revelation" that has enlightened them. Instead of "making points" for you as you might expect, then, it only hardens them in their convictions. It is frustrating to find an unassailable fortress where we most want to expose the faultiness of their position.

In almost every instance a member of a cult lives a highly compartmentalized life. In many cases they have very few or perhaps no serious points of contact with reality and the world. Although living in the same world and among the same realities that we all do, they make no meaningful contact with it, for their beliefs have removed them from such considerations. They may be "sent" into the world, but it is always as evangelists, never as learners or participants in that world. One possible exception might be the Unitarian-Universalists, if one considers them a cult.

Discussions with members of cults expose yet another generality that becomes a rule: They are pretty well conditioned as to just how to respond to outside contacts. Casual conversational exchanges may bring standardized responses. It surprises many people to find such conditioning prevalent, but membership in a cult requires conditioned responses almost to the point of where each one sounds almost as though he/she were a carbon copy of another.

Most bewildering to people who engage members of cults in discussion is the strong conviction they have of having been "freed" from "religious exploitation" by their association with the cult. Since outsiders see them as enslaved, it comes as a shock to find that they consider themselves the most free of all people. Such conviction lies deeply imbedded in the cult mentality. The leader or founder of a cult or its authoritative writings have convinced followers that they have been liberated from all oppressive forces of orthodox religion and that only within the confines of the cult can they dedicate themselves to the free expression of what life is all about.

Lastly, it is virtually a universal truth that the cults are all highly disciplined within the framework of their own thought system. That may sound like a truism that need not be stated, but it extends beyond their beliefs into a highly disciplined life-style that is often challenging to a nonmember. By "highly disciplined" we do not mean merely a life-style morally in keeping with what we think of as "straight" or "uptight" or "clean," but rather a life-style fashioned upon their faith with rigorous enforcement as a total way of life. The demands and requirements of such a life-style are frequently spelled out in great detail by the leader of the cult and followed with rigor.

2

Why the Surge of Cults in Our Day?

Cultural Factors

Many factors in today's culture seem to have given rise to the uncommonly large number of cults. We can speak only briefly and superficially of a number of them here, but we hope such a preliminary discussion will help readers understand the task of the church as we attempt a meaningful approach to members of these cults.

The Dominance of Feeling Over Intellect

Of great significance is the increasing dominance of the "authority of feeling" over the "authority of intellect." By this we mean that it has become far more important to know how you *feel* than to know what you *think*.

Some of this is a result of a certain anti-intellectualism that has followed the high hopes that were once placed on technology and science. Only a few years ago disciplined thought held great hope for giving the world a bright future, but today we have a world filled with more problems than before. Whether thinking can solve the problems of the world or not has become a major question. Many people are convinced that thinking creates more problems than it solves.

Since thinking, especially scientific and technological thinking, attempts to manage the things that can be seen, by analyzing them and controlling them, the reaction to this has been to place more emphasis on what cannot be seen. Our feelings belong to us alone. Other people can mold our minds to *think* a certain way, but nobody can make us *feel* a certain way. So it is more important for us to know how we feel than to know what we think. This line of reasoning has made a huge impact on today's world.

To understand life, then, is to look inside yourself to find out what is happening within. Thinking requires that you look outside yourself for the most part, trying to figure out what is happening around you. If you look inside yourself, you are beyond anybody's control. If you look around you and try to relate to your surroundings, you are subject to someone else's control. Nobody but yourself has the last word about your inner life, while many others exercise controls that restrain your external life.

The feelings that you uncover within yourself, then, are neither good nor bad. They are just the way you are, and it is important to know, through such introspection, who you are and how you feel. Nobody is to tell you how you "ought" to feel, for that would only be to say how someone "thinks" you should feel. You need not feel one way or another to be good. Essential to your self-understanding, though, are your feelings themselves. And this can be carried to such an extreme that one is frequently under the distinct impression that it is more important to *feel* well than to *be* well.

Whether you find serious flaws in this way of thinking or not (and, to be sure, there would appear to be very serious flaws!), this mood pervades today's world. And if a cult can promise good feelings to people who have

11

gotten tired of being made to "feel bad" by the way the "thinking people" manipulate and control them, the person who wants to "feel good" is set up for membership in a cult.

The Mood of Relativity

"Nothing is sure. Everything is relative." Statements such as this dominate today's world. The sense of being in a world where one can never be sure of anything has come partially through science, which seems to uncover new things all the time that seem to contradict old and indisputable facts once held with absolute certainty. If even scientific fact proves to be relative as new knowledge is acquired, why should there not be equal uncertainty over against things we cannot see—such as religious truth?

When the mood of the times shifts from "logical thought" to "feeling" as described above, the difficulty of maintaining stability in long-held truths is still greater. The truths of old were said to have been based on a "revelation," something given to man from outside his experience of living. However, a person "feels" religion more than one "thinks" it. And religion sinks to a subjectivity that depends largely on what "feels right" than what "is right" or what "appears to be right" by external processes of logic. So the sense of relativity bred in scientific effort is strongly reinforced by today's mood that depends on feelings.

When there is nothing one can count on anymore, nothing sure about life, a sense of insecurity sets in. It is difficult to live with too much uncertainty, and virtually everything around the 20th-century American seems to be unstable. It is as though we were floating on an open sea of uncertainty with nothing to guide us, nothing to give us direction, nothing to assure us that we are going in the right direction toward a secure tomorrow.

If such a sense of insecurity becomes too great for a person to bear, one quickly starts looking for at least one or two things that he/she can be "sure" of. If a cult can convince somebody that there is "certainty" within its enfolding arms, that one can easily become victimized. Even if the "certainty" seems a bit strange or weird or different, it can easily be explained because everything about today seems strange and different from any previous age. Why should there not be a new revelation, a new way given for the person of today to follow? It almost seems appropriate, since the rest of the world has gotten so far removed from its past in such a very short time, that new religious forms should also emerge that are significant deviations from the past.

So the ties of the cults to the past, combined with deviations that seem to make them so much a part of the present and future, are highly attractive. In this way the strong personalities and their "revelations" have an allure in keeping with our day. And if they can enfold a person in such a way as to make the person "feel good" and at the same time give him/her a sense of security in an uncertain world, the cult has a new adherent without too much resistance.

The Need for Human Community

A person needs to feel wanted. Loneliness is devastating to the ordinary person.

Yet loneliness is one of the most pervasive feelings in the people of today's world. American society in particular has placed great stress on individual achievement and the importance of individuality. The cost has been loss of a sound sense of community among people.

Loneliness, of course, is as old as Adam and Eve. Sin immediately put a wall between them and then also became the occasion for the first murder as Cain was pitted against Abel. Sin always isolates one person from another, and such isolation inevitably leads to individual acts that rupture the human community. Sin always leads to a life of private desperation as one person is cut off from another.

The need for human community has always been an intense drive, however, and throughout the ages man has been able to devise ways to live meaningfully within a common community. Accommodations had to be made, of course, for individual self-understandings, but life together always was more meaningful than life in isolation.

Today's population explosion, however, has made it harder and harder to know many people intimately. When society was organized around tribes and small communities, everyone knew everyone else. They may not have been special friends with them, but they knew the people with whom they lived their daily lives and had a common bond with one another. What was good for one was good for the other, since their mutual good depended on the welfare of the society they shared.

It is all but impossible to know everyone in the communities in which most people live today, and one must pick and choose friends from a variety of possibilities. But there are so many people with whom we must relate, at least casually, that there is less and less opportunity to relate strongly to a smaller group that gives us a sense of belonging, a sense of security and permanence.

This sense of security and permanence is further hindered by the high mobility of society. One knows that friendships are quickly broken up by moves made either of necessity or by choice. It is risky to get too close to someone else, for he or she may move on. Better to fend for oneself, even if it is a lonely way to go.

Then, too, it is an axiom of the day that if you don't look out for yourself, nobody else will. This leads on the one hand to a distrust of others since they may take advantage of you rather than help you, and on the other hand it leads to a sense of fulfillment if you can live a ruggedly individualistic life. The "self-made" man is one to admire. So you are admired if you cut yourself off from other people at least to the point that you never depend on them. You can run with them and party with them, but don't depend on them. In short, don't develop community!

In these and many other ways that could be mentioned, Americans of today are more and more isolated from one another and they long for the "old feeling" of belonging, of being a member of a "caring community" where wounds can be bandaged and happinesses can be shared.

The cults are bound together into tight-knit communities. One of their most marked features is the way the members of the cults are deeply conscious of their interrelationship. They draw their life in the cult from the community within which they move. A deep sense of commitment is coupled with obvious caring for one another.

Again the phrase echoes in our ears: "The cults are the unpaid bills of the church." The needs of our time have raised the framework for the establishment of the cults just *when* and *where* the church should have been hearing and responding to a need. Anyone who has a "handle" for reestablishing a sense of belonging and community has a very real edge on gaining people's allegiance in our culture. The cults have laid hold on this need, and their success shows how deeply the need is imbedded in today's world.

The Rise in Leisure Time

Most people deny they have more leisure time than ever before. They will claim, in fact, to be busier than ever.

That we are indeed a busy people does not mean that we have no more leisure than ever before. It only means that we have filled time once spent in "survival busy-ness" such as planting and sowing and harvesting with "leisure busy-ness" such as children's dancing lessons and golf and membership in clubs. However defined, by standards of only a hundred to two hundred years ago we have far more leisure time than any generation before us.

The fact that we find it so imperative to fill our leisure time with a new sort of "busy-ness" may be of great significance. For without being busy we are confronted with a void, a sense of purposelessness, a feeling of "what's the use of it all?" Even in the middle of our "busy-ness" such thoughts cross our minds. But with less to do for survival, the chances increase of such thoughts crossing our mind in idle moments.

The question, "Am I happy? . . . REALLY happy?" becomes a dominant question. And we seek happiness with a passion because the question has had a chance to surface in ways it never could when life was a struggle merely to survive.

Under such circumstances the stress on feelings mentioned earlier begins to take its toll. All too often we find ourselves less than satisfied with life as we live it. Being surrounded with plenty has by no means made for a full and satisfactory life. It becomes downright frustrating, in fact, to find that we have practically everything we could ask for and yet want more. It is even more frustrating to find ourselves unable to say what more we want, what it would be that could make us happy. We long for something we cannot identify and hope passionately that someone will tell us how to find it!

Again the cults have found a way to get at this passion for happiness and self-fulfillment. They know very well the importance of a person's being strongly committed to a cause in order to gain a sense of importance, of being needed. And happiness lies in this direction rather than in the direction of comfort and wealth.

The church must hear the phrase over and over again: "The cults are the unpaid bills of the church." The words of Jesus call for commitment and offer meaningful opportunities for service, but somehow the church has often failed to communicate what the Biblical message has made clear, and the cults have filled the void.

The Authority/Freedom Struggle

A peculiar paradox of our time, already mentioned in passing, is the tension between the need for authority and the drive for freedom. What is the proper place for the exercise of authority? How can one be free and yet subject to enough authority to keep order in the world?

Much depends, of course, on how one chooses to define words. The word "freedom," e.g., is made synonymous with "licentiousness" by many. Thus defined, it removes all restraint and gives full sway to the rule of one's feelings. "If you feel like it, do it!"

In a much more responsible way, though, "freedom" is far different from "licentiousness." It holds in tension a sense of responsibility and the opportunity to choose a number of options. So it reflects on the question of where restraint is necessary and where it is an infringement on personal right of determination. It is willing to ask what is necessary for the common good and how one's personal options may be used to the end of that common good. Only within that frame of reference is the question of "what I feel like doing" to be asked and answered.

Authority, likewise, must be exercised with something of the same restraint. It, too, must be exercised in behalf of the common good rather than at the whim of personal advantage. Authority needs as much restraint as does freedom. Neither is an absolute; each must be held in tension against the other.

The tension between the two has been seriously tested in our day against the background of the pressures we have mentioned. In their extreme manifestations, the advocates of freedom cry out against almost any kind of authority and the advocates of "law and order" seem to be willing to exercise authority almost without any respect for personal rights and freedom.

So who is to say what is right and wrong? Where and how and by whom is authority to be wielded? When and why and under what circumstances is it to be resisted? Children are reprimanded for "sex outside of marriage" and yet see in their adult models a promiscuity that causes them to question the authority by which they have felt their lives circumscribed. So they become a "law unto themselves," "doing as they feel" without regard for the admonitions expressed by "authorities."

With such a breakdown of understanding, the question of religious "authority" is also raised. On the one hand, an argument can forcefully be made that faith is purely a private and individual matter. The argument goes: Since nobody else can believe for us, then nobody else should be able to tell us what to believe.

If faith is indeed subjective in this way, there can be no truth. For if truth is whatever you want it to be, it can never be identified or passed on. It is only whatever you personally "feel" to be right. Authority is meaningless in religion as well as in life.

Over against this the question must be asked if there is not a place for "authority" in religion. Truth has substance to it, and it is affirmed by the experience of the ages. It needs interpreters and teachers who have been disciplined by its force. The claims of "revelation" on the lives of religious people always have the ring of "truth given from outside our own subjective opinion."

Since cults function with a strongly authoritative mentality, it is important for us to recognize these tensions of our day. When people are left in their "freedom" to believe what they want to, they often find themselves in a confusing wilderness of ideas. If/when somebody convinces them that there is something definite to be known and live by, a religious conviction that is given "from above," the ground is prepared for membership in a cult.

Once more the church must ask how it has failed in the task of keeping authority and freedom in proper tension. These are questions that have been at the heart of Christian understandings throughout the ages, and yet somehow the whole problem has slipped through the fingers of the church in recent years. Cults have prospered where they have been able to exhibit strong authority with an accompanying sense of giving freedom to the person who submits to their authority. The times have provided the framework for the appearance of such cults.

Religious Factors

The cultural factors seem to open the door wide for the advent of the cults all by themselves. Add to them several important religious factors of our day and you have an even more inviting scene for the surge of cults.

Shallow Religious Understandings

There is a notable lack of serious and deep knowledge of Biblical content among members of American churches today.

The Biblical message undergirds many of our cherished American ideals and heritages. This is not to say that our country has ever been distinctly "Christian" in the sense that this kind of understanding was written into our governmental documents. It is to say, however, that even those who were not Christian were much influenced by certain Biblical thrusts in the past history of our country.

These thrusts are watered down and frequently lost today, not only among those who are professedly non-Christian but also among those who *do* confess the Christian faith. Knowledge of Biblical understandings is superficial and minimal among people of most denominations today, to say the least.

Churches such as the Lutheran and the Roman Catholic in which a period of instruction is offered for the children may have a little stronger understanding of the Biblical message, but even among them one can rarely speak of a well informed adult understanding of the faith.

If one's understanding is stunted at the level of a child with the assumption that it contains the full depth of what the faith has to offer, there is not much one can expect by way of dialog with a cult member who is thoroughly indoctrinated and completely sold on the faith system he/she represents. A child's faith will not be able to stand up to such an assault. It may just cave in (as it does on some occasions) or it may simply retreat and run away (as it does on most occasions), since it becomes terribly threatened by the obvious fact that the member of a cult has an incomparably greater understanding than the member of a church.

This lack of understanding may be due in part to a need for greater knowledge of Biblical content. It is a deeper problem, however, for one needs to know some basic principles of *using* the Bible, apart from being aware of its overall content. This is a problem much too large to go into here, but training people in the proper use of Scripture is equally as important as helping them gain proper knowledge of its content. The cults that have Biblical roots are guilty of doing peculiar violence to Scripture by the way they use it, but most Christians are very inept in countering such misuse through a proper awareness of how to handle it properly. On occasion such ignorance makes them easy prey for the cults. Far too little time is spent even in those churches with rather extensive instruction periods on this particular aspect of Biblical understanding.

The Meaning of Life

One of the most difficult questions one can ask is this: "What is the meaning of life?" The Bible can, on the one hand, answer rather simply in terms of loving God and our neighbor, but it can also reflect a deep awareness of how complicated such an answer is.

Without question, this is a basic inquiry of our time. It is answered in many ways by many people, some saying the meaning of life is found in conquering all suffering and trouble, others saying life's meaning is found in the acquisition of possessions, and still others relying on the old answer that life's meaning lies primarily in loving. Many answers can be found to this age-old question. More and more, the answers are changing from materialistic to spiritual and transcendental answers.

Yet, for all the answers around us, despair continues to reign. Our answers ring hollow in our ears, and loving is found to be harder to perform than to talk about.

The church proposes to have at its disposal the key to this answer in its proclamation of the Christ. But somehow its message has either gotten garbled so that it is beyond understanding, or else the church has not been about its task at all. Instead of proclaiming its message boldly and forthrightly, it seems more often to have followed the trends of the time and couched its message in terms that seem to be quite unclear to the world.

The cults have stepped into this void with the boldness that the church should have had and have seized the opportunity. The upsurge of astrology, e.g., is directly related to this quest for meaning. It puts the meaning of life into a large universal setting and has blended personal meaning with universal meaning into one system of thought as ancient as the world itself and yet as modern as the sciences!

Some cults are content to deal with such problems on lower levels. Getting a person through the next day, whether he/she has any sense of purpose at all, is the minimal intent of a movement such as Transcendental Meditation. Although TM has no answer to the meaning of life, it at least is able to help a purposeless life through its day-to-day struggle. And many people will gladly settle for that!

This quest for meaning has far-reaching implications and springs from many aspects of today's world. The church cannot ignore this search, and the cults are plain signs to the church that it must take the inquiry seriously.

The Need for Personal Involvement

One result of the search for "the meaning of life" has been a new stress on personal involvement. Participation in society in general, or in a "crusade" of some sort, may be a way of acquiring meaning for oneself.

Yet activity may not in itself be a *search* for meaning. It may be a sign that a person has found something he/she considers worthwhile enough to merit full attention and energy. The type of activity will often reveal what has given meaning to a person's life.

This, of course, is the hope and intent of the Christian faith. Once God's claim has been laid on life, it is intended to change the entire direction and thrust of one's activity. Christian faith is a commitment to full involvement in life on new and different levels.

This type of involvement has a highly social dimension and makes demands on a person's total life-style.

The cults, however, stress still another dimension of involvement, one that relates to our earlier discussion of "community." When one is committed to a faith system, one is at the same time committed to the body of fellow confessors. It is plain to the members of the cults that they cannot hold a "faith" without a "supporting community."

Thus it is imperative that they become involved in a gathering together, a community, a mutual coming together for the common good of all as well as for one's personal good. It is hard, if not impossible, to be marginal members of the communities that gather in cultic ways. One must be involved deeply in the common life of the cult.

Sometimes such involvement may be liturgical and ritualistic in form, such as in Hare Krishna. Sometimes such gathering is in the name of social welfare, as is typical of the Black Muslims. At other times it may be in a "save the world" activity, such as the years voluntarily given by young Mormon men in evangelistic efforts.

The involvement affords the "security" and sense of "being wanted and needed" that are necessary for people who move from this kind of internal involvement with their own community to the more "risky" and "dangerous" involvement of relating to the outside world.

Whether involved within the community or in engagement with the world, a sense of fulfillment and satisfaction is available to the participant. And this sense of fulfillment is vital to the ongoing life of the cult.

Such a sense is a very religious need and again alerts the church to the fact that it cannot merely call to faith without also calling to life. Involvement within the church and involvement in the world are at one and the same time important to the life of the Christian. This involvement must be meaningful and vibrant, however, for people soon see through merely playing meaningless games and calling it involvement. The cults have taken a deeply running religious need and have made the most of it.

The Wide Appeal of the Cults Resulting from All This

We have tried to point out in each instance how these various facets of today's religious and cultural life provide a built-in door through which the cults enter. Some use one entrance and others another. Not all use the same stress or fulfill the same needs. But the vast multiplication of cults today indicates that many needs are waiting to be met and that many cults are waiting to seize the opportunity.

Since the cults have obvious attractions to people of our day, it is important to point out that the members of the cults by and large derive great satisfaction from their participation in such groups. This is not to say all are "happy" in the way we frequently use the term, but many people are more content to be "satisfied" than they are to be "happy." Their satisfaction lies in feeling that they have found a place in life, a meaning to which they can attach themselves. And usually that is the source of a "happiness" in itself.

This is important to say because one is tempted on occasion to try to convince a member of a cult that he/she is not really "happy." This temptation is particularly great if one happens across a member of a cult with a complaint of some sort. But such an approach is counterproductive. The members of the cults are members precisely because they have found certain needs met and have found satisfaction in their associations with the cult. Any attempt at convincing them of their "unhappiness" will be a dead end. They will quickly assure you that in spite of any complaints they are "happier" or more "fulfilled" than they have ever been before.

It is likewise a poor approach to attempt to point out the "irrational" nature of the cults. Since most of the cults have an authority system with some form of special revelation undergirding their beliefs, such arguments will get one nowhere. They consider such an assault on their system as one born of ignorance, since an outsider cannot possible understand what it means to be a member, with all the benefits that are derived. Members of a cult are content to let the "irrationalities" stand without question.

Inasmuch as the cults foster a strong sense of what is right and what is wrong, clearly delineating these things in their system, one could speak of an idealism that appeals to the members. The surrounding environment, as we have suggested, speaks of relative truth, relative morality, even a relative future, depending on which courses we decide to take in our present decision making. This seems to present a rather cloudy picture for one who wants to live by strong ideals. If nothing is certain, how does one make decisions? And the cults answer with the strong systems of authority and morality that present clear-cut areas for decision making and living. This idealistic desire for clear-cut answers appeals to many as they join the cults.

The "study of the future" has become a field of concern in our day. The future seems so uncertain in the light of the options we have. "Far out" ideas get hearings they would never have had in another age. Science fiction is an example of the kind of hearing visionaries and dreamers can obtain today. And they are frequently taken with far more seriousness than were the creators of "Buck Rogers" only a few decades ago.

In this milieu, also, the cults find comfortable ground to stand on. Even "far out" ideas can obtain a hearing, and if they are coupled with other ingredients that blend just right, they can almost inevitably find followers. And if the cult can also project something of a possible future alongside another "far out" idea, so much the better . . . and so much the more appealing to many people!

Here one can see in the Christian sects how powerfully such "future thinking" has become. People like Hal Lindsey have laid hold on prophecy/fulfillment themes and have projected the future in imaginative ways (supposedly based on Scriptural motifs, but using very questionable methods of Biblical interpretation) and have captured the imagination of large portions of today's church.

How powerfully, then, can the new revelations, the new approaches, the new prospects, the new projections of movements like the Moon cult and the teachings of Maharaj Ji speak to people of our day!

Interestingly enough, the very "persecution" of the adherents of the cults has a positive appeal to their followers. To be persecuted for the right is one of the strongest driving influences that can seal a person into a movement. If one is convinced that he/she is committed to "truth," and if that "truth" is rejected by an outsider and the outsider even makes life difficult for the proponent of truth, it is proof positive that the forces of evil are trying to overturn the forces of good. Thus every attempt to discourage their approach only strengthens their conviction. We often look at the way they make such a nuisance out of themselves and wonder how they dare to be so obnoxious. It appears to us that they must surely get discouraged with the way people in general treat them. We become apologetic about how on occasion we have had to become rude because we had to do something to get rid of them. We are sure we have offended them and hurt their feelings.

On the contrary, the persecution and mistreatment often maintains an intensity of commitment among them that daily fires their zeal. For it is the persecution that proves how right they are!

In Summary

It is apparent from the above analyses ... and these have only touched the surface . . . that there are many historical, cultural, psychological, sociological, religious, and other factors that stand behind the proliferation of today's cults. One cannot simply pass these phenomena off as unimportant. The church can, in fact, through these factors find clues that will help gain a better point of entry into the lives of those who live in the latter years of the 20th century.

3

Understanding the Cults

The Development of Cults

In examining the origins of the cults, certain generalities may help explain what happens as we encounter them. If our own understanding of them can be deepened, it may be possible to find points where we can communicate with them if we can muster the patience and will to do so.

As with any generalities, there are always exceptions to the rule. Trite though it may sound, it is important to acknowledge this from the beginning.

In general, the cults have sprung up around a powerful and overwhelming personality. They are rarely grass-roots "popular movements" of the people. Without Mary Baker Eddy it is questionable whether Christian Science would ever have gotten off the ground. Without the drive of C.T. Russell it is doubtful whether Jehovah's Witnesses would ever have achieved any sort of status. Some are pure personality cults, such as those of Father Divine a few years back and Maharaj Ji today, while others have gone past that and have developed into full-blown movements.

Where the personal influence of a founder or driving force was lost through death and a movement developed in his/her wake, there is almost inevitably some sort of authoritative writing that has come from the hand of the founder or early leader. Such writing(s) becomes the interpreting filter through which all subsequent activity of the movement takes its shape and form. The "grass roots" following of such movements has little to say about its development. Those entrusted with interpreting the unfolding movement according to the writing(s) of the founder direct such development and growth.

A second generality that has some exceptions is one that was mentioned earlier in this booklet but which needs particular emphasis at this point. Usually the cults represent a "heresy" of some religious faith that has a mainstream of orthodoxy, whether Christian or some other religious system.

This is where it becomes particularly important to know something about where the original founder "came from." If you know that, it will often be helpful toward understanding where they intend to "go."

It is helpful, e.g., to know that Joseph Smith had been a Freemason and was subsequently removed from the Masonic lodge. That helps explain some of the Mormons' ritualistic structures.

Or again, it is helpful to know that Moon has a Christian background in the Presbyterian Church in Korea, from which he drifted into Pentecostalism and anti-Communist activities.

Likewise, it is helpful to know that millennial thought has a long history as a peripheral position in the Christian church from the earliest times and is not merely a recent movement.

Current adaptations of thought to older forms of religious expression stand behind many cults, and the more you know about the background of a cult's founder the better equipped you are to understand what the cult itself stands for. To understand a "heresy," in other words, one must also know what the original orthodoxy is. Thus understanding Hare Krishna without knowing something of Hinduism, or understanding Baha'i without knowing something of Islamic thought and eastern religious understandings, is all but impossible.

This gives aid, in turn, to understanding "community." Most cults are very tight-knit groups. Closeness of community in almost every instance originally centered on the personality of the founder. It is likely, in fact, that the "founders" of the cults rarely had many followers during the early part of their career and perhaps never knew significant success within their own lifetime. Small groups committed to a leader, however, are almost without exception extremely close to one another.

The question, then, is how this original closeness is fostered and maintained after the death of the founder. He/she must have built something into the fabric of thought that lives on, something in which lies the key to the continuing life of the group. For there are many cults that die with the demise of the leader. What provides the new center of unity in those that live on, so that the fellowship can be maintained and grow?

The obvious center to which members of a cult will be attracted is the writings that convey the understanding of the leader who originally served as the focus of their fellowship. They will on occasion even vest such a person upon his/her death with messianic character, thus giving reason to continue their fellowship within a context of worship and adoration.

The writings of the person, of course, usually receive an expansion and take on a life of their own through interpretation. Such activity usually requires an authority structure of some sort, since someone must be authorized to say what is and what is not a proper interpretation of the writing. Such a structure is seen plainly in groups like the Mormons, whereas other loose-knit movements may develop a number of "centers of interpretation" and split into many factions. However, apparently freethinking groups such as the Unitarian-Universalists may have surprisingly strong leadership in national headquarters. Written interpretations of prior writings and/or current developments will almost inevitably be found for the ongoing fellowship of the cult.

This maintains in turn a sense of closeness and "orthodoxy" of their own making. It also clarifies any truth that may seem obscure for the fellowship, and moves within the authority/freedom polarities we discussed earlier. "Interpretations" must be made for each age succeeding the death of the founder, and on occasion "developments" may even become necessary. So a rather rigid authoritarianism and set mode of transferring authority emerges before very long, if a cult is to continue.

Thus provision is made for the continuation of the original message with any developments or interpretations necessary for those who follow. Orthodox belief systems and patterns of life become regimented, and membership must always be "initiated" into these systems in some way. Originally the basic commitment may well have been primarily to the person, but over the course of time the commitment becomes more and more to a rather rigidly established and interpreted set of teachings and life-styles. Yet such developments and interpretations nearly always have their point of reference in the original founder and his writing(s) or those writings that may have come from his immediate successor who claimed authority.

This sort of development may on occasion lead to division and separation between groups. The Reorganized Church of Jesus Christ of Latter Day Saints is an example, for it stands in opposition to the Salt Lake City group of Mormons over certain essentials that came into question after the death of Joseph Smith.

Any such development of "orthodoxies," of course, calls for a continually more detailed formulation of definitions and phraseologies (although the founder may have begun such a process already before his/her death), which quickly becomes deeply encrusted with meanings unique to that cult. This is the "double-talk" we mentioned earlier, for the combination of words and phrases rooted in orthodox usage and then redefined through the development of the cult leads to a whole new dictionary of meanings for old and seemingly well-understood words. One cannot assume too much in the way of common understanding even of familiar and time-worn words and phrases.

The Cults Encountered Within History

When we encounter the cults, they are usually either well on their way to becoming full-blown movements or have already matured in many of the ways mentioned. As we see them, then, there are a number of marks we are almost certain to find. Among such marks might well be the following:

The cult as a system will very likely be rigid in belief and life pattern. This is what makes dialog and/or direct approach so difficult. One must be prepared for hard work and much frustration, equipped with much patience, if any exchange of understanding is to take place. This is not to say such an exchange is impossible, but it is to set it into the perspective of hard work. The rigidity of their systems creates special problems that must be reckoned with.

Rigidity is necessary for their existence, however, and we must recognize this. Should any "crack" in their belief system ever appear, it would in itself be enough to cause the whole structure to tumble down. That is the danger of the "authoritarian" approach, attractive though it first appears. They sense this intuitively even though they may never have consciously thought it out, and therefore they will not permit anyone the opportunity to "crack" the certainty of the system with all its interlocking parts. There dare be no room for doubts or questions. The cult has "truth" in a most certain form. It is to be proclaimed, not discussed.

"Listening" on the part of members of a cult, therefore, is a form of politeness. If you insist, they may be quiet for a while as you explain your point of view, but quietness is not the same as "listening." They will "hear" only such things as they can answer with certainty. Given the floor again, they will frequently proceed as though nothing had been said. "Conversations" become monologs with possible interruptions on your part that must be tolerated in order to give opportunity for their proclamation of the "truth."

When thus encountered, one cannot but be impressed with the

dedication and commitment found among members of the cults. Their task is all-consuming. Their faith is untouchable by doubts and uncertainties, and they are knowledgeable about their beliefs.

This commitment is solidly grounded in the authority system of the cult, whether it be the original personality if he/she is still alive or whether it be the system of writings that have developed in the cult's maturing. Nonetheless, cult members will frequently appeal to an authority with which you are acquainted, particularly the Bible if they spring from rootage in Christian traditions. Jehovah's Witnesses, e.g., will rarely appeal to the authority of their own cultic leaders or C. T. Russell, their founder. They will rather have you reading the Bible (in their own translation, however, which is the only true translation by their standards). The explanation will frequently sound rather good if not actually familiar, for they will be using words and terms the Christian has heard before and with which he/she is at least vaguely familiar. But the effect of the "double-talk" mentioned earlier starts taking its toll if one is not careful, for the familiarity gives way to confusion and then a terrible feeling of uncertainty about one's own ground of faith. The ground is then plowed for their sowing of the foreign seed of their faith.

The faith system so planted has a way of life enfolded within it that affirms their dedication. The member of a cult who approaches you will not merely speak a word but bring a style of living that affirms the depth of his commitment to the message he/she brings. The Armstrong cult, once known as the Radio Church of God but now actually forming local congregations, will immediately be recognized by a long string of regulations that keep the whole of life in check. To the casual observer many of the things involved in such life-styles seem absurd and unintelligible. To the member of the cult they are not only "explainable" but are integral to the faith system. It is part of the witness itself to make the life-style unique and identifiable as being born and bred by a "living faith."

The life-style frequently seems "out of touch" with reality as ordinary people experience it, and because that is true, it is frequently the nonmember who raises the wall against dialog rather than the member of the cult. One shies from "getting caught up in" such a foreign way of life, after all. The nonmember is prone to writing off the member of the cult as a "weirdo" or a "kook" and closes the possibility of understanding or dialog from the beginning. That is why such pains have been taken here to show how totally integrated the faith and life of cultic members is. If we understand this, we will have a bit more patience and will be more willing to at least tolerate, if not understand, some of the behavior and faith patterns that seem so strange to us. Only then will we be able to seriously engage in discussion. It is of little help to isolate members of the cults even more than they already are.

This is not to say that our mere understanding and patience will open dialog possibilities. The "evangelistic forays" of the cults into the world are not to discuss, but to proclaim. The members who come to us are not very interested in exchanging ideas, and it is of great importance to them that they keep themselves separate from the world even as they enter it. So they rarely try to hide the "strangeness" of their ways inasmuch as the "strangeness" is itself a part of the witness as well as a defense against the

24

world that may try to "change" them.

This becomes a vicious cycle, of course. Those who are deeply committed to the cults will never permit their faith-system to be exposed to alternative ways of thinking nor their lives to be exposed to alternative styles of living. They will, in fact, insist that they "know" about such alternatives since they once were enslaved to such systems. Now that they are "free" they do not need to further expose themselves to such corruptions and they resist such exposure. So they become more and more deeply enmeshed in the very perceptions that cut them off from the reality we are trying to communicate to them.

The intense devotion to "evangelism efforts" is probably the mark by which most people identify members of the cults. Rarely are the members seen within the confines of their own community, since it is closed and tight-knit. Only on rare occasions may an outsider be admitted. Contact is nearly always on the level of their "evangelistic encounters" with the world.

Evangelistic activity is very important to the cults. One would not want to take away the integrity of the member by insisting that he/she has any motive other than the promulgating of the truth of the cult itself. In his/her mind the primary motive will be to win others to the cause of the cult and the "truth" it promotes.

There are other factors involved, nonetheless. Some are more plainly evident than others. Some are perhaps more consciously recognized by the members than others. But we must draw attention to such things as these:

Most of the cults (again with some exceptions) have intense requirements for such activity built into their "membership clauses," if one can call them that. The commitment of all Mormon young men to dedicate a portion of their lives to evangelistic activity is typical of such requirements in many cults. Such requirements are not merely contractual fulfillments. They are "training periods" in preparation for a life of such activity, where and when possible.

Beyond the requirement level, however, such activity is important as a form of "protection" from the questions and doubts that so easily come on a person given to introspection. Granting that this reason for strong stress on evangelistic efforts would be vehemently denied by the cults themselves or the members who are engaged in the efforts, the simple fact remains that evangelistic activity shelters a person from introspection. For an outgoing, persuasive task such as the evangelistic endeavor keeps you confidently repeating the very things you yourself need to be convinced of. The more you repeat these truths, the more they are ingrained within you. The more deeply you are involved in such a persuasive task of convincing others, the more convinced you will be yourself—without a single moment to introspectively question the truth of your proclamation. This "protectiveness" of the evangelistic enterprise is of great value to the cult and is one way it has of maintaining high involvement and commitment on the part of its members. It could never live purely on its own inner resources alone. Any weakening of a member in evangelistic effort is immediately recognized by the cults as a weakening in total commitment to the cult's faith and life. A close watch is immediately set upon such a person, for there is a concern for keeping him/her in the cause.

Yet another result of the strong evangelistic thrust of a cult is the effect it has of getting its members to "prove themselves" to each other and to the authorities. It does more, in fact, for it is even a *"self*-proof," an affirmation of one's own convictions. Such proving of self in peer groups and with authority figures is an important part of maintaining one's position in the close-knit community. It is a powerful way of affirming one's own strength of commitment to the cause. Such a combination of factors, by which one's own self-worth is maintained, one's place in the community is assured, and one's dedication to the cause is proved, makes the evangelistic work a very integral part of membership in the cults.

Were the cults content to believe something in private and to live in monastic societies, most people would think them "quaint" but rather "harmless." It is the combination of factors just described, however, that stirs most people first to irritation and finally to opposition. It must be remembered, in spite of our irritation and opposition, that their evangelism efforts spring from the very reasons why they associated with the cults in the first place. Until we realize this, we shall miss the point of their efforts and write them off without ever attempting to address them.

The point of this booklet and the others in this series is to stress the simple fact that the church cannot just write off the cults any more than it writes off any group of people. The good news of Jesus Christ is for members of the cults no less than it is for the church. So we must now turn to our own self-understandings in an attempt to see just how we might approach the cults and what can be said to them.

4

The Marks of the Church
Against Which the Cults Are to Be Tested

When members of the one holy Christian and apostolic church in general and the Lutheran Church in particular encounter the cults, certain very specific things need to be kept in mind.

Resemblances Between the Cults and the Church

It is disturbing upon reflection to find that so much of the way the church appears to the world is mirrored in the way the cults appear to the church! It is probably apparent by now that there is only a thin line between the marks of the cults and the "marks of the church." Consider such things as the following:

When we say that cults find their original thrust to have come from a person rather than from a grass-roots movement, only later erecting an authority structure to maintain, preserve, and promote the teachings of the original leader, we must remember that is exactly how the church began! There was no grass-roots movement in Judaism that became known as Christianity. There was a man named Christ, whose life and teaching became the center of the religious thrust eventually known as Christianity.

It is no wonder that the church was originally considered nothing but a cult by Jewish and Roman authorities alike. Its focus on one Man who had deviated significantly enough from orthodox Jewish teachings that they had found it necessary to crucify Him was the mark of a cult. Little did they dream what a movement was beginning! The original concern of Jewish authorities was to keep the general populace from being "contaminated" with these deviant teachings, and the concern of the Romans was to stamp out a pesky cult that conveniently bore the brunt of a Roman backlash at the time of the burning of the city. Christians were considered expendable, and Roman authorities needed a scapegoat to blame for the disaster. With the blessing of Roman and Jewish authorities alike a "cult" was put under persecution with the expressed purpose of wiping it out!

Since they were considered criminal by the established government, early Christians had no choice but to meet secretly. They developed a strong community life, with caring and concern being vital to their life together. A worship life drew them together, and a liturgy began forming that gave a universality even to their local gatherings. They could not be shut up even under persecution and were known for their strong evangelistic emphases. Finally they became known as people who "turned the world upside down," and their efforts undermined the very stability of the Roman government. Nobody gained entry into their inner circle save members alone, so apart from their evangelistic efforts little was known about their main teachings. Rumors abounded about what terrible things they did in their meetings.

They developed a series of authoritative writings that became normative for all their teachings. Particular stories and understandings became filters for "orthodox" teaching and practice. No wonder the Jews finally "closed the canon" of the Old Testament Scriptures at Jamnia in 90 A.D. No more "authoritative books" were to be added, for a Christian Scripture was emerging and threatening to merge with the "orthodox" Old Testament books as authoritative for Christian teaching. It was felt that this would severely distort Jewish teaching if it were permitted. So the way of safety for the preservation of Jewish understanding was to close their list of authoritative writings to further additions.

Meanwhile the intensity of the Christians' life together was common knowledge. While not many knew the specifics of what happened among them, it was generally realized that they were very much a part of a family, an accepted part of a new community of close-knit believers. It was generally said that they were bound together in love and their talk was regularly of care and concern.

This can be said in various ways of the cults today. And that is why we suggested at the beginning of this section that it is a disturbing thing to church members on occasion to reflect on the close resemblances between the origins of the church and the cults as we see them today.

The stress on "orthodoxy" in the cults has its counterpart in the church. For the church has always recognized that where there is truth there is also the possibility of falsehood. If one teaching is "orthodox," its opposite or a contradictory teaching must be "heresy." We need not be surprised that the cults stress "orthodoxy" so much.

Nor need we be surprised at their stress on commitment, for again the church has always recognized a call to firm commitment in the Scriptures. We as Christians have a specific commitment to a faith and life that calls on us to respond from the deepest part of our being to its hope and promise. There need be no surprise that the cults also call their members to deep commitment.

The evangelistic fervor itself is an understandable echo of our own commitment to spread the Gospel into all the world. We may disagree with tactics, but Christians do not disagree with the idea of or need for evangelism efforts. If our zeal has diminished from that of the early church, it is not because the Scriptural injunctions ring out any less clearly. We are called to proclaim the good news of Jesus Christ to people everywhere. Such an emphasis in the cults is not surprising, for where people are convinced they have "truth," they are also convinced of the need to proclaim it clearly.

So a shadow haunts the church as it examines the cults. The church sees something of its own history in them!

Questions Raised in the Light of This

Since there is so much about the cults familiar to us and since within our own history there was a time when the Christian church was considered a cult, how can we or dare we *judge* the cults? A number of major religions have risen in "cultic" form out of previous religions.

We have mentioned the Christian church as one. Islam was originally considered a cult combining Jewish and Christian "unorthodoxies." Buddhism began as a cult in Hinduism. Who is to say, then, that a cult may not become a major world religion and become recognized in its own right? Some of the cults today are showing remarkable "staying power," with growth surpassing that of the Christian church, percentagewise. The Church of Jesus Christ of Latter-day Saints is a virulent cult that promises to become a religion in its own right, related to and yet distinct from Christendom. Others are pressing in the same direction. By what right, then, do we judge the cults to be wrong and rouse ourselves to dialog with them or to "evangelize" them in return?

Or, on another level, how is the church distinguished from the cults, since they seem to share a number of overlapping marks? Do we not mutually show a common intent of benefiting the world through the promotion of our faith? So why "fight" one another by trying to "convert" one another? Since many ask such questions, we need to face them squarely.

In short, what is to be the position of the church over against the cults if it does not become their judge? Are we to simply forget them since they show no interest in dialog? Are we to ignore them and hope they will go away? Are we to persecute them as opponents of the truth? Are we to aggressively seek to convert them to Christianity? Our own members are being approached by them, and we need to deal with these questions in some way.

It is such questions that have called forth this booklet and the others in this series. In order to gain the perspective needed for answering them we must now review very quickly some of the central marks of the church. In this way we will see not only the crossovers and similarities, but also the distinguishing and unique features of the church itself in the conflict with the cults. By force this is the quickest of reviews, and readers are encouraged to pursue this part of the study on their own at greater length within their own churches.

The Marks of the Church

The primary mark of the church has always been considered a right and proper use of Scripture. This sounds simple enough as stated, but volumes are written on what that implies.

Many people mean by this emphasis on the centrality of Scripture that it alone has authority for teaching and doctrine. Many cults will agree with this. And then Christian people are at a loss, for if there is agreement on the authority of Scripture, how can there be such vast areas of disagreement?

Of course, this makes the cult sound like a denomination with the primary problem being one of interpretation. One must, therefore, search further, and before long one will in most cases find a "key" to interpretation, a basic writing that is itself the authority by which Scripture is to be interpreted. So Mary Baker Eddy's writings become the basic authority by which the Scriptural Word is to be understood. The basic authority is then discovered in reality to be a writing quite other than Scripture itself.

Not all cults will speak so openly of Scripture as the authority, however. Non-Christian religious cults, of course, do not so claim, and even some of the cults with Christian rootage may speak of it only as one authority among others. The Mormons will openly admit that Scripture is not in and of itself an authority outside of other revelations and writings they have.

There is more to it than merely a question of authority, however. As was mentioned much earlier, the methods and principles used in interpreting Scripture are also vital keys to distinguishing the church from cults. We suggested that "a *right* and *proper* use" of Scripture has been considered the primary mark of the church. Just what does that imply?

It is more than a question of interpretation alone. There have always been differing opinions and understandings about certain difficult portions of Scripture. Denominations are a testimony to centuries of uncertainty and dispute about the meaning of certain parts of the Biblical writings. In our own day denominations have internal disputes about what kinds of methods and principles are admissible for dealing with such interpretational questions. There is nothing new or cultic about this kind of an argument.

What is generally agreed upon when considering Scripture as the primary mark of the church, however, is that the writings of the Bible belong to the whole church. In other words, Scripture is not and can never be used in a purely "private" way. One person cannot simply say "Scripture means this" or "Scripture means that" on the strength of his own authority. Even in churches where strong personalities have been behind their founding, such as Luther in Lutheranism, the word of Luther alone is not sufficient to establish the meaning of Scripture. Scripture belongs to the whole church and needs the balance available through the common understanding of many Christians.

Even with the denominational differentiations, then, the common understanding of the church is confessed through creeds and confessions where the universal truths are acknowledged in the middle of the individual differences.

Cults deviate significantly from norms such as this and instead go into paths dictated largely by the whim of a leader or founder who has intentionally separated him/herself from the main body of the church.

There are many other aspects of this "mark of the church" that should be considered, but let this suffice for here to show the point where cults and denominations differ in their use of Scripture. A multitude of problems continue to attach themselves to just what is meant by the "right and proper use of Scripture," but those are problems that you can work through within the framework of your own study in your congregation.

One other thing might be mentioned, however, in connection with Scripture as "authority." Such a statement presupposes the authority of the *whole* of Scripture. While the use of proof passages is helpful in things like catechetical instruction, it has some dangers built into it. It gives the impression that the Bible has little passages to give answers to any questions one may raise.

When, therefore, a member of a cult comes with a multitude of "proof passages" for his case, it confuses the Christian who has been instructed by such methods in his earlier years of catechetical instruction. Valid and valuable as the use of proof passages may be, they can never in themselves be the whole of Biblical study or knowledge. Themes and motifs and broad backgrounds of understanding are also built into Scripture. To attempt to isolate such themes in the form of little passages is not possible. When cults use passages in this way, the listener must be on guard. Abuse of Scripture rather than proper use of it is a very real possibility at times like this. Again here the churches themselves are frequently at fault for trying to conduct theological education in such shortcut fashion as to give the impression that one can capture the Scriptural teachings by learning a few isolated passages. This is an area along with the others mentioned that needs to be pursued in the studies of your local congregation.

Alongside the proper use of the Word of God the church has always considered the proper administration of the sacraments equally important as a mark of the church. Baptism and Holy Communion are, of course, intimately tied to the Word from which they gain their meaning and efficacy. But wherever the Word is rightly taught it has always been understood that the sacraments are going to be properly administered.

There may be many "sacramental images" and reflections of such practices among the cults, but the very abuse of the Word we have discussed makes a "sacramental presence" of the sort we speak of a matter of nonimportance among them. The right use of the sacraments is one of the marks by which the church is clearly distinguished from the cults, regardless of whatever practices, rituals, and enactments we may find among them.

There may be overlaps at this point, as in the Mormon "baptism for the dead" rituals. Where such are found, one must return again to the basic foundations of the Word itself. By contrast with the cultic practices it will quickly become plain that their intention is far removed from the Christian intention in the use of the sacraments.

Again we stress Peter's urgent call, from which we have taken the title for this series of booklets: "Always be prepared to make a defense to any one who calls you to account for the hope that is in you, yet do it with gentleness and reverence" (1 Peter 3:15 RSV).

To follow this directive of Peter we need to know what our own faith is all about as well as what the faith of the other person is about. That is part and parcel of our intent in these booklets.

But above all it is important that one see past the teachings to the humans who carry the teachings. For it is not to teachings that witness is given; it is to the people who themselves stand in need of God's saving grace that Christians are called to give an account of their faith with the same commitment and faithfulness with which cultists bear their witness.

5

What We Can Learn from the Cults

Lest we think this study is an exercise in futility, let it be said that even if it does not help us in successfully dialoging with a cult member, it can certainly aid us in seeing ourselves from another perspective. We can learn something of what we can be doing in today's world, what the needs of our world are, what kinds of images we want to project to the world as we go about our task. Such a learning process by looking at ourselves through a back door, as it were, can hopefully aid us in being more faithful servants of the Lord.

Yet this way of looking at ourselves can also help us in opening doors of discussion with the cults themselves. It is to be hoped that the following suggested list of things we can learn from them will help us also to approach them with better understanding and new possibilities for dialog.

What, then, can we learn from what the cults have shown us in regard to our own time?

A Reflection Worth Reflecting On

As a beginning thought we might ask ourselves if we speak of our own faith winsomely, as something that fills our life with meaning and joy, or is our own witness one of sour-pussed necessity? Do we "with gentleness and reverence" conduct our lives in such a way that people wonder what "makes us tick"? Do our "evangelism campaigns" in our own communities look and sound like the approach of concerned and caring people, or merely a hopeful swelling of numbers in church? Is our life-style reflective of deep commitment? As we watch and reflect on the way members of the cults make their witness, we are called in turn to reflect on how our own witness can best be made and heard.

A Lesson About Authority

"What *is* proper use of authority?" That question is important simply because the church does proclaim an authoritative message. To give witness to the Scriptural truths is to give witness to a revelation that we all consider a norm for teaching and life. And within the church itself life is conducted with an understanding of authority, whether it be the family and home or the church and society.

Authority is a universal need. Anarchy cannot long exist without sucking into its vacuum an authority of some sort by virtue of a deeply felt human need for order. The cults well understand the *need* for authority. The church must reflect on how best to testify to an authoritative Word and how best to organize authority within its own family of believers at least if not also in the larger society of mankind in such a way as to leave maximal freedom after necessary authority has been exerted.

The Nature of Doubt and Questioning

There is a "confidence" among members of the cults that is so unassailable as to appear to be a mock and a fake. This is not a judgment, but a reflection of what one can commonly hear expressed in a statement such as, "Who could possibly believe so confidently without one serious doubt? It's all a front and a fraud!"

This should give the church pause for reflection about the place of questions and doubts in the face of faith. It would hardly be appropriate to laud doubt and encourage questions as though there were merit in this. Yet it is unrealistic to think that we can ever have a faith free of doubt so long as we live in a world where sin surrounds our life. Where the Evil One is at work, doubt lies close at hand. Superconfidence that refuses to confront doubt seems less than real to people who daily wrestle with questions and uncertainties.

To be sure, an "alive faith" is always reflecting on what it sees and hears. It is constantly subject to winds and clouds that come into and blow through our lives. Reality is by no means a simple thing to deal with. This need not surprise us. It is the common lot of mankind.

As faith goes through such a process of reflection on the reality it experiences, it will have questions and doubts, whether it wants them or not. Those who are strongest in the faith are those who can bend with such assaults and still stand tall. Denying them is only to be less than honest.

If we have learned that doubt is part of the experience of every person, we need not be ashamed that we have our questions even while we do not boast about them. Our witness will not be afraid to surface our own doubts if/when this helps to make it more credible. We will not deceive others into thinking we have never had a doubt. We will, on the other hand, make our witness credible by proclaiming the certainty of Christ into the very teeth of many uncertainties, all of which we have taken into consideration and are free to talk about.

This is not so strange inasmuch as the holy writers were always willing to express their doubts and questions to God with boldness, for in so doing they "tested," as it were, their faith against God and let His gracious Spirit win them.

This is very different from tempting God, from placing oneself deliberately into the path of unbelief and challenging God. That is a misuse of the faculties God has given us and is different from expressing doubt.

To recognize the realities around us, though, and to be willing to express the questions that are raised as we reflect on life is to join with the whole of mankind in a common bond of experience. And against that a firm statement of conviction concerning Christ's resurrection and the promise of God's grace rings with a new sound. It is not just the hollow voicing of a word *we* have chosen, but it becomes the proclamation of the Word given to us in and through that One whom God has marked as His Chosen One through the Resurrection and Ascension.

Commitment and Dedication

Few will deny that we can learn something about commitment and dedication from the members of the cults.

On the one hand we may well learn *not* to let our commitment become one to a pastor, a denomination, a cause. Our commitment is always and above all to Christ. It is all too easy to shift our focus of commitment without realizing it when we get caught up in side issues and lose the heart of our faith. In observing the cults we do well to learn again the importance of keeping our commitment strongly centered on the grace of God in Christ.

On the other hand we can learn from the cults a lesson that we need to learn over and over again, that we are called to be confessors of Christ's name in both word *and* deed. The dedication of life that is related to the confession of His name is part and parcel of what it means to be Christian. The cults show us again that confession and life-style go hand in hand.

So the cults call us to renew for ourselves questions such as these: Does our community hear from our lips the name of Him whom we confess to be Lord and Savior . . . and does our community see in our lives a dedication to Him whom we confess? Does our commitment seem almost cultlike in that we devote ourselves to a church or pastor or denomination, or is it plain that our commitment is above all to the Lord who has called us in Jesus Christ to serve Him?

Sound Biblical Study and Knowledge

Since we have mentioned this at some length earlier, we will not dwell on this point here. But it needs to be forceably emphasized again that the church must help its members gain a better and fuller understanding of Scripture far beyond a mere "prooftext" knowledge of its content. Help must be provided in knowing how to use and interpret Scripture in its larger emphases as well as offering a better understanding of its message. Until members of the church are willing to engage in a serious study of things like this, the cults will find far too ready an ear in the very backyard of the church itself.

The Place of Doctrine in the Church

Along the same line we need to recognize the place of doctrine in the life of the church. Doctrine is not *merely* "a place to stand," "a point of reference for those who want to know what we believe," "a position to present that others can take or leave as they will." Doctrine does indeed tell where the church stands, but it is much more.

Doctrine is an orderly way of presenting the fulness of the living Scriptures within the context of a contemporary setting. It attempts to order the teachings of the church as found in the Scriptures in such a way that they can properly be brought to bear on contemporary questions. Were it not such a constant struggle to re-present the old truths to new settings, we could simply repeat the doctrines as stated in the second century or the 16th century and be done with it. The continued wrestling with how to present these teachings to today's world in meaningful fashion is the sign that the Scriptures are always in contact with an unfolding and developing world. So one does not merely repeat old statements as though they made sense in every age. They are constantly reworked and restated to meet new needs.

The cults show us what happens when statements of teaching and faith become rigid and no longer "bounce off" the world around us. They are splendid examples in many cases of doctrine that is formulated without serious contact with the world they intend to address. From them we can learn how important it is for the church to remain in touch with both the authoritative Word from which we derive our teaching and the world which we intend to address with our teaching.

This is not to say that doctrine will necessarily *adapt* to the world with concessions and compromises. The doctrine of the church may well contradict the world as it unfolds. But it must always be in touch with that world and must speak to the concerns of that world. It is not merely a repetition of teachings once stated in another context.

Far too frequently the church looks cultic in the way it handles the presentation of doctrine. From the cults we can learn how *not* to be, so that we can truly present a living doctrine to a living world.

Toward a New Sense of Community

A major need of contemporary man, as we have said earlier, is to find a place where loneliness can be overcome and a sense of belonging can again be established. The cults have shown the church what a strong attraction such a community of people can be. That the cults are growing and flourishing is undoubtedly attached to a large extent to the fact that they have capitalized on this intense need for human community that virtually everybody feels.

The church is intended to be just such a place! Any casual reading of the New Testament will reveal a purpose related to caring, concern, acceptance, love, support, and other such marks of human community. When the church reaches out in compassion for those who are tortured and tormented in body and soul with a support system that can enfold people with any type of need in the name of God and with His grace in hand, it will be what it is meant to be. And God Himself will be in and with such activity, bringing healing and wholeness to the world.

Such a community will truly make sense to the world that the cults are now reaching with such obvious success. The church can and must learn the lesson of the magnetic quality of community as a support system for lonely people. The Mormons above all have shown the place community has in a faith system. The church should not be afraid to learn some important lessons from groups like this on the level of life together in the community of God.

The Need for Experience Coupled with Knowledge

The church need not fear "experiencing the faith." Where there is a strong emphasis on "knowing" the content of God's revelation, the church must be called back from time to time to a realization that knowing does not automatically surrender the possibility of experiencing the presence of God.

The cults have created some interesting blends of knowing and experiencing. The church may learn something about how to combine the two, for humans do not live merely by knowledge. There is a mystery about life that defies knowing. It calls for experiencing life, drama, vision, and "otherness" about life beyond our seeing. The church dare not neglect this part of its responsibility any more than it can neglect its responsibility to instruct in what knowledge is given to man by God.

In short, the church must recapture something of the mixture of mystery and knowledge that comprises its faith. The cults have shown that it is not only possible, but an important ingredient of life.

35

Evangelism in the Shadow of the Cults

The cults attract many people with their commitment, zeal, and enthusiasm. In our day there is so much apathy, so much wishy-washy lack of commitment to anything of consequence, that it becomes almost refreshing to find someone strongly dedicated to a cause and a faith. More than one member of a cult has joined precisely because of such apparent zeal.

At the same time many people are repelled by an overextension of this zeal and enthusiasm on the part of the members of the cults. They are frequently more guilty of "bad taste" than they are of outright rudeness, but they quickly gain a reputation for running roughshod over the feelings of anyone who engages in discussion with them.

Again the church can learn from the cults. On the one hand the enthusiasm and zeal and commitment of the members of the cults should be the hallmark of Christian people, who have exciting things to get enthused over and committed to! All too frequently it is precisely the *lack* of qualities like this that make our Christian witness seem to fall flat. People wonder why we don't act more enthusiastic and dedicated if the faith is everything we say it is. A vibrancy of faith that infects all of life is a very important aspect of our Christian witness.

The warning we must take from the cultists, however, is the warning against going beyond good taste. There are times and places where we do well to take into account the situation and realize that it is not the best environment for witness. Witnessing for Christ is a very important part of our faith, but that does not mean that every time and every place is equally good for exercising that responsibility.

It may well be, in fact, that some of our witness has been dampened because the very word "witness" makes us think that we are supposed to imitate an eager Jehovah's Witness knocking on doors or a pushy member of a cult making him/herself obnoxious by the way he/she presents his/her case.

This means, in short, that we dare never let a negative image of witnessing to the faith give us reason to shut down our own witness, and yet we are called to exercise reasonably good taste in all we say and do as Christian people.

6

Attitudes to Be Encouraged Toward Cults

"Always be prepared to make a defense to any one who calls you to account for the hope that is in you, yet do it with gentleness and reverence" (1 Peter 3:15 RSV).

Attention is called to this passage for more than one reason when encouraging proper attitudes to be fostered over against the cults. The obvious reason is because the passage encourages us to do more than passively receive whatever is being taught by the cults. We are urged to "be prepared to make a defense" to them.

The passage is stressed for still another reason. It encourages Christian people to make their defense of the hope that is theirs "with gentleness and reverence." In the face of the temptation to rudeness and impatience, the admonition to remember the person with whom we are speaking as beloved of God is important. No matter how much the teaching a person brings upsets us, we are reminded to remember that the person bringing it remains important to God . . . and therefore to us. So we are to deal with such a person in all "gentleness and reverence." With encouragement to this end we conclude our booklet.

Some "Don'ts"

Gentleness and reverence dictate some don'ts as well as some things to do. We will begin with the things to avoid, and then speak of the positive possibilities for Christian witness as our final word.

1. *Don't be hostile.* Members of various cults may consider you their enemy, but this should never be part of a Christian's "defense system." They as people are not an enemy to be conquered. They are fellow humans who need Christ. This must be kept clearly in mind.

2. *Don't slam the door in their face.* Not even "with gentleness and reverence"! This does not mean one will never be firm with them, make an appointment with them at a more convenient time, insist that one has a schedule that must be met after a reasonable time, or other such ways of maintaining one's integrity. This can be done "with gentleness and reverence." But slamming a door in their face without respect is not in keeping with gentleness or reverence.

3. *Don't argue heatedly.* Logic will not prevail. It must be remembered that the members of the cult work with a revelation and authority quite foreign to any that the average church member will recognize. But a heated argument only affirms for them their own rightness! It does not win points and it will lose them if you are trying to be a point-maker. Heated arguments, like slammed doors, do not lend themselves well to "gentleness and reverence."

4. *Don't show anxiety.* If you understand their background and you know your own faith, having done your "homework" well before their visit through faithful use of God's Word, you will not have to worry about making a fool of yourself. You can ask intelligent questions and make intelligent responses. Anxiety almost inevitably encourages them to

assault you. It will rarely raise their sympathy in your behalf. Be calm and cool in your own witness. If they can be confident, you also can be confident if you are properly equipped with an understanding of your own faith.

5. *Don't rely on yourself alone.* It should go without saying, perhaps, but let it remain central to your preparation for such encounters: Pray for the Spirit constantly. He has promised to stand by you and give you the strength of His presence. He will lead you and guide you if you are willing to be His servant and seek His guidance. Any lack of success, as one may repeatedly experience, is not a sign of an absence of the Spirit. He has promised to be near, and His promise can be relied on. With Him near, one is "always prepared to make a defense to any one who calls you to account."

Having stated these negatives, it is important to present oneself in a positive way to those who witness in the name of the cults. Such a positive witness on our part involves at least two elements . . . the gift of patience and the gift of love.

The Gift of Patience

When schedules are hectic and time at a premium, the most difficult of all gifts to give a person is patience. Yet that is part of the "gentleness and reverence" Peter calls for.

What has been said up to now has been an attempt to foster some sort of understanding of the people who have become involved in the cults and what such an understanding means to the church. Where such understanding prevails, there may be room for a bit more patience than if they simply appear to be "weird" and "strange" to us.

To understand members of the cults in terms of their fervent commitment may be of some help. One need not get impatient with them for having a commitment. Our concern is not that they have a commitment, but rather that the commitment to which they hold is destructive to their own well-being in spite of what they believe so strongly. Commitments in themselves are not bad, but a commitment to the belief that touching live electric wires will not harm a person does not stop death. One can honor a commitment. The concern is that the person is committed to something that is destructive to his/her welfare.

One can understand their commitment to authorized sets of writings in general, or the authority of a person in particular. Christians have the Scriptures and Christ. They know how important authority is and how central a Person can be to faith. Understanding the importance of such things may help gain some patience in dealing with cultists.

Understanding can also be expressed when the underlying set of "doctrines" to which they hold is exposed and discussed. Christians, too, have such. They can patiently permit members of a cult to have "doctrines" without getting upset over that fact.

The cults' drive to evangelism, also, can be honored and respected. Christians share the need to proclaim the Good News. So one must not make light of a commitment to evangelism. Cultists can point right back at us and ask us why we think it is so important and then deny them the right to do the same. Their enthusiasm and zeal can be honored even when we disagree with the direction it takes.

In short, our patience can be helpful in granting them integrity in their own right. We can then understand that we are not to push on them in ways we ourselves do not want to be pushed. If we do wrong to counter a wrong done to us, two wrongs do not make a right. We must give them the honor that we would expect to receive from them even when we feel they have wronged us first. That calls for patience—a patience not easily come by, but one that is "gentle and reverent."

The Gift of Love

If we are to be patient with them on one level, we are to be loving with them on another level. The "gentleness and reverence" to which we are called requires that we be concerned about them with warm genuine concern. We are not to see them merely as a statistic that would look good on the church roster. ("A converted Jehovah's Witness! Oh, wow! ! !") Nor are we to see them merely as "things" to be manipulated by pulling the proper strings and repeating appropriate Bible passages to them. (This is the objection to their approach, that their lack of listening turns people into "things" to be manipulated rather than people to be loved.) To attempt, then, to manipulate them, in turn, to a "satisfactory" faith stance (namely, our own) is less than a genuine concern for them as people. The cultists are human brothers and sisters who are just as sinful as we are and as much in need of Christ as are any of us who call ourselves by His name. Their total welfare is a matter of our own continuing Christian concern. Rather than treating the members of the cults as one feels that he/she has been treated by them, it is imperative to treat them *as one would have them treat him/her* if their approach were genuinely concerned about the welfare of other people.

Our love for them, in other words, is born of the patient love of the God who has first found humankind in the Christ. "Love" can always be twisted and warped, wanting to "manipulate" rather than wanting to be truly concerned, wanting to use love to get one's own way instead of letting love open the lives of others to the potentials God has set before them. Realizing all this very clearly and recognizing at the same time how the pure love of God has renewed those very people whose warped love has used others, one will always try to view the members of the cults with this love born of God. This will help deal with them through "the eyes and heart of Christ."

That may on occasion, as it did with Christ, mean that we have room for disagreement and sometimes even anger. But it will mean that we always keep in mind that the cultists are creatures from the hand of the same Lord who is the common Father of all, and that they need the same Christ who died for the world. Seen in this way, they will be transformed and one's patience will be joined with deep love for them. Then one will be better equipped to deal with them in all "gentleness and reverence."

In love such as this, those who have joined the cults will be known in the fullest sense as brothers and sisters. Their needs will be joined to the needs of all men. Their hurts will be common with humanity. Where they have been deceived, they will know the companionship of all people who are subject to being deceived.

Then deeds and discussion and contacts with them will be performed in truth and patience and love rather than in haste and spite and malice. For they will be seen as people with needs common also to those whose needs have been satisfied by the loving hand of the Christ. Then it will be possible to speak and act under the direction of the words of Peter: "Always be prepared to make a defense to any one who calls you to account for the hope that is in you, yet do it with gentleness and reverence" (1 Peter 3:15 RSV).

Bibliography

Breese, Dave. *Know the Marks of Cults*. Wheaton: Victor Books, SP Publications, 1975.

Martin, Walter R. *The Kingdom of the Cults*. Minneapolis: Bethany Fellowship, Inc., 1965.

Robertson, Irvine. *What the Cults Believe*. Chicago: Moody Press, 1966.

Starkes, M. Thomas. *Confronting Popular Cults*. Nashville: Broadman Press, 1972.

Van Baalen, J. K. *The Chaos of Cults*. Grand Rapids: Wm. B. Eerdmans, 1938.